ALPHABET ZOO

Pat Chapman & Martha Ellis

Copyright ©2021 All rights reserved.

No part of this publication may be reproduced, distributed, or transmitted in any form or by any means, including photocopying, recording, or other electronic or mechanical methods, without the prior written permission of the publisher, except in the case of brief quotations embodied in reviews and certain other non-commercial uses permitted by copyright law.

978-1-7398104-3-6 (Paperback)
978-1-7398104-5-0 (e-book)
978-1-7398104-4-3 (Hard Cover)

Printed in the United Kingdom

AEGA Design Publishing Ltd
Kemp House, 160 City Road, London
EC1V 2NX United Kingdom
www.aegadesign.co.uk
info@aegadesign.co.uk

 is for
ALLIGATOR,

Look!
He's smiling
at you
Alligators live
in swamps,
Hidden by thick,
green goo.

B is for
BISON,

**Big, shaggy and brown.
Found on the open plains,
They make snorting sounds.**

 is for

CHEETAH,

The swiftest animal on land.

 is for

CHIMPANZEE

With feet that are used as hands.

D is for
DOLPHIN,

A small and friendly whale, Jumping and playing in the ocean, Using its rudder-like tail.

E is for
EAGLE,

Known for keen,
sharp sight.
This symbol of
America's freedom
Is powerful when
in flight.

F is for
FROG

Watch it jump
and hop,
Sometimes
basking in
the sun
Or lying
on a rock.

G is for GIRAFFE

The tallest of quadrupeds,
With a very long neck,
two small ears,
And four spotted,
ladder-like legs.

H is for
HIPPOPOTAMUS,

Swimming in
the muddy river.
Opening its
super-sized
mouth
Will quickly make
you quiver.

I is for
IGUANA,

Scurrying on the ground, This large, tropical lizard Is usually green or brown.

J is for
JELLYFISH,

**Lazing
in the ocean.
You can
almost see
right through it
As it floats by
in slow motion.**

K is for
KANGAROO,

With its long tail and wide pouch,
So mother can carry her baby
As it snoozes or looks out.

L is for
LEMUR,

Jumping from tree to tree, Alert with eyes open wide During his nocturnal spree.

 is for
MEERKAT,

Standing tall and
always aware.
They love
to play in
family groups,
But a guard will
always be there.

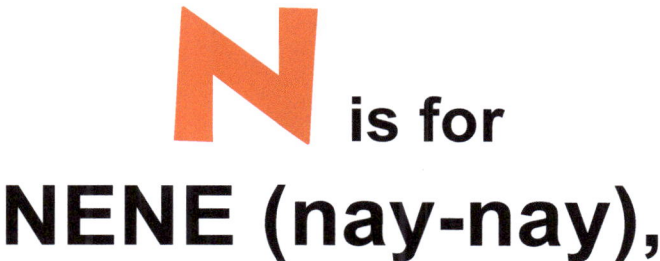 is for
NENE (nay-nay),

The state bird
of Hawaii.
This world's
rarest goose
Is found on Kauai
and Maui.

O is for OWL,

A wise old bird,
Always asking,
"Who?"
Listen! Have
you heard?

Who-o-o...
Who-o-o

P is for PENGUIN,

**With happy-feet
in the snow,
Waddling in
a camouflage suit
That looks like
a tuxedo.**

Q is for QUAIL,

A small,
short-tailed bird,
Plump like
a soccer ball
Scratching the
ground for food.

R is for
RHINOCEROS,

**With a large
horn and
very thick skin,
A nose that alerts
of danger
While sniffing
in the wind.**

S is for SHEEP,

With fluffy
coats of wool,
Following
the leader
Like we do
at school.

T is for
TIGER,

The largest of all cats, With dark stripes on red-orange coats To camouflage their backs.

U is for
GNU (new),

A large African antelope, With a very long head, a mane, And a beard, much like a goat.

V is for
VULTURE,

**Soaring high in the sky,
With binocular-like eyesight,
In groups they often fly.**

W is for WARTHOG,

Kneeling low
to dig for food
With tusks like
an elephant
And looking
rather rude.

X is last letter of
FOX,

A wild dog that's cautious and sly,
With a pointed face and bushy tail,
And a howling, scary cry.

Y is last letter of BUTTERFLY,

Drinking deeply from each bloom, As it flits from flower to flower, Delivering pollen in return.

Z is for
ZEBRA,

With stripes of black and white, Looking almost like a horse Better able to stay out of sight.

Now, you are learning the alphabet with real animals to help you begin.

Let's go back to the letter A and do it all over again!

LAGNIAPPE

ALLIGATORS have up to 80 teeth at a time, and throughout a lifetime, they can have 2,000-3,000 teeth as new teeth grow to replace worn ones.

BISON can run 40 miles an hour and jump 6 feet high.

CHEETAHS are cats that cannot climb trees. They hunt their prey by day and only drink water every 3-4 days.

CHIMPANZEES spend much of their time grooming each other, tickling each other, and hugging and kissing each other. They often make up games and activities to entertain themselves.

DOLPHINS, because they are mammals, need to come to the surface of the water to breathe. Dolphin mothers have been observed nestling and cuddling their young.

EAGLES return to the same nest every year, repairing and adding to it each time. This remodeled nest has been known to grow to 8 feet wide, 15 feet tall and weigh 2 tons.

FROGS in a group are called an "army". Frogs don't drink water with their mouths; they absorb it through their skin.

GIRAFFES only sleep 10 minutes to 2 hours a day...usually standing up. The patterns on giraffes are totally unique (which means no two giraffes are alike).

HIPPOPOTAMUSES are considered among the most dangerous animals in Africa. Hippos lounge in the water by day and graze for grass in the night. **IGUANAS** can detach their tails if caught and then grow another.

JELLYFISH are boneless, brainless and heartless.

KANGAROO babies look like pink, hairless worms when they are born and are the size of a jellybean. There are more kangaroos than humans in Australia.

LEMURS have flat fingernails similar to humans. The tail of a lemur is longer than its body and can be used for balance as well as communication.

MEERKATS always have one sentry on guard to watch out for predators while the others forage for food. Varying signals are given to alert the clan to head to the burrow or just crouch low until danger passes.

NENE (nay-nay), Hawaii's state bird, is a goose found on all islands of Hawaii...and nowhere else.

OWLS have three eyelids: one for blinking, one for sleeping and one for keeping the eye clean. An owl's ears are different sizes and at different heights on the head to assist in superior hearing.

PENGUINS can stay under water for 10-15 minutes before surfacing to breathe. They swim so fast they can propel themselves 7 feet above water. All penguins live in the Southern Hemisphere from Antarctica to the Galápagos Islands.

QUAILS are considered ground birds. They can only fly a short distance and usually are found walking. Quails bathe in the dust to keep their feathers clean and to keep pests away.

RHINOCEROS adults have skin up to 2 inches thick. They soak in mud for hours a day to protect their skin from biting pests and blistering sun. Rhinos can weigh 2000-6000 pounds. Still, they can run 28 miles an hour... and only run on their toes!

SHEEP produce about 8 pounds of wool in a year. When sheep have a haircut, it's called "shearing." One pound of wool can make 10 miles of yarn. (Note: There are 450 feet of wool yarn inside a baseball.)

TIGERS are cats that cannot purr. Instead of purring to show happiness, a tiger will squint its eyes or close them completely. Closing its eyes translates to "I feel very happy when you're here, and now I can relax."

GNUS (news) are noisy animals. They constantly emit low moans and, if disturbed, they snort explosively. Gnus are also known as wildebeests.

VULTURES, when threatened, vomit to lighten their body weight so they can escape more easily in flight. Vultures are birds that do not have songs. Instead, they are limited to grunts, hisses and bill clacks.

WARTHOGS are very fast runners. When they run, their tails stick straight up in the air. Warthogs bow on their padded knees to graze and dig for bulbs and roots.

FOXES have vertical pupils, similar to a cat, helping them to see well at night. Foxes use the earth's magnetic field, like a guided missile, when hunting. They are playful animals that have been known to steal golf balls from courses.

BUTTERFLIES taste with their feet since they don't have mouths. Instead, they suck food up with a kind of drinking straw called a proboscis. Also, the eyes of butterflies consist of 6,000 lenses.

ZEBRAS have stripe patterns that are different for each individual, making them as unique as snowflakes and human fingerprints. Zebras care about each other. When one is wounded by a predator attack, other zebras will circle the injured individual and attempt to drive the predators away.

ABOUT THE AUTHORS

Retired educators Martha Ellis and Pat Chapman, in the recent phases of their lives as photographers and writers, continue educating as they share their international encounters with people, animals and places.

Earlier books of such experiences include *Journey to the Seventh Continent*, about their expedition to Antarctica, and *They Laugh In My Language*, filled with photos and poems revealing the common threads of mankind as seen through the expressions of children.

100% of the profits from their book sales go to a foundation for the education of children.